Real Life Fantastic Beasts and Where to Find Them

A Didcot House Publication

I0417511

Real Life Fantastic Beasts and Where to Find Them

A remarkable centuries-old publication buried in the heart of the New York Public Library has lately been revealed to the wider world. This monumental work, originally compiled in the 1600s by Dutch historian Arnoldus Montanus (1625-83) collected the stories, maps and observations of dozens of explorers to the New World of the North and South Americas and Australia. Translated into English in 1671 by the well-known cartographer John Ogilby, the following are selected extracts from these tales of ancient travellers that concern the fantastical creatures they encountered on their voyages and where such creatures could be found.

AMERICA

Chimeric "Monster" in Brazil

Extract from The Voyage of Vincent Agnes Pinzon (Vicente Yáñez Pinzón), 1499. Location: Brazil

He got sight of the Parian coast, and with admiration beheld a tree which sixteen men could not encompass. Between the trees he saw as strange a monster, the foremost part resembling a fox, the hinder a monkey, the feet were like a man's, with ears like an owl , under whose belly hung a great bag, in which it carried the young, which they drop not, nor forsake till they can feed themselves.

Dining with Giants in Curacao

Extract from The Expedition of Americas Vesputius (circa 1497). Location: Curacao

The next remark in this voyage was the discovery of an island where he found the footsteps of a gigantic people. Nine Spaniards went a league to search the country, where they saw five great huts, standing in a spacious valley, and in them two old, and three young women, each of them being twice as tall as an ordinary man. The old ones invited the Spaniards to eat, who when they were sat down, consulting how they might take and carry one of these giantesses to Spain, there to show her for money, thirty six giants came in to them, (never did the sun shine on a more terrible people) which so amazed the Spaniards, that their hair seemed to stand on end at the fear thereof.

Every giant was armed with a bow and arrows, and a club. They, wondering at the nine strangers, stood talking very earnestly one to another, which gave the Spaniards time to think of making their escape. Some judged it convenient to discharge their guns upon them, and in the smoke to run away; others thought that it would be better to take a milder course, which they all agreed on; and taking their leave went out of the hut, but were followed by the giants, who kept a stone's throw behind them, and went faster or slower, as the Spaniards slackened or quickened their pace. At last getting to the shore, and from thence into their boats, the Spaniards suddenly put off; but the giants then pursued them with eager speed, all of them leaping into the water, and swimming, shot an abundance of arrows after them; but frightened by the thunder of two great guns that were discharged from the ships, returned ashore, and fled into the neighbouring hills.

Tree of Madness in Codego

Extract from The Expedition of Alphonso, Fogeda, Diego Nicuesa, Ancifus, and Roderick Colmenares. Location: Codego

Americus Vesputius was scarce fitted out in Lisbon, when Fogeda set sail with three hundred men from Beata, the main haven of Hispaniola, to the Island Codego, inhabited by naked people, but of comely personage, and withal expert and most excellent archers. Here he found a very strange tree, which bears a fruit not unpleasing to the palate, yet deadly poison, and besides, whoever chances to sleep under their shadow, loose both their understanding and eye-sight, and never attain to their former senses, unless they take some opiates, just as dangerous, and so by a long sleep, recover.

Plague Trees in Panama

Extract from Peter Arias (Pedrarias Dávila) his Expedition, and Remarkable Passages of Vascus Nunnez (Vasco Núñez de Balboa). Location: Coiba, Panama

The neighbouring territory Coiba produced trees, whose timber used for shipping never breeds worms, because of its acerbity; whereas on the contrary, all other vessels in that country are very subject to that inconvenience. Here also grow those famous Plague Trees, whose very leaves, if but falling upon one, are like Gods Arrows, mortal, and immediately kill, unless the place on whereon they light is straightaway anointed with fasting spittle: and the Coibensers say, that they know another poisonous wood, which they use to destroy their enemies withall.

Columbus Doesn't Eat the 8-Legged Serpents of Cuba

Extract from First Discoverers of America. Christopher Columbus in America, 1493. Location: Cuba

He next discovered Cuba, which sailing round about, he found also to be an island; where landing in a convenient harbour, on each side fenced with a high and jutting rock, he espied two little hovels, wherein was abundance of fish, besides two great snakes or serpents, each having eight feet, spitted, and ready to be laid to the fire to be roasted; but neither man, woman, nor child to be seen, they being gone with part of the fish they had dressed, into the adjacent woods; whither the Spaniards following, saw hanging by small strings, on the branches of trees, abundance of snakes, some of which had their mouths tied together, others their tongue and teeth pulled out.

CHRISTOFEL COLONUS.

Hence marching on, a little beyond they saw a company of the natives, which they judged to be about seventy men, covering the top or summit of a hill, to whom the Spaniards made signs, and to entice them near, showed several of their gaudy trifles; but in vain, till at last one adventured, descending from the hill, to whom one of the natives (who in the first voyage that the Admiral made, was taken from the Island Guanahaini near Cuba, carried to Spain, and there christened) called aloud, telling him they need not fear, they should have no harm done them; which said, they came down all together, and informed them, that they were sent by their King to catch fish for another King, which was with him at dinner, and if they had not eaten the serpents, they gave them many thanks; for they were provided for the second course, and very scarce to be got, being a greater dainty than any fish.

Columbus from hence proceeding on further westward, discovered a fruitful coast, verging the mouth of a river, whose water runs boiling hot into the sea. Somewhat further he saw very strange fishes, especially the Guaican, not unlike an Eel, but with an extraordinary great head, over which hangs a skin like a bag. This fish is the natives fisher; for having a line or handsom cord fastened about him, so soon as a turtle, or any other of his prey, comes above water, they give him line; whereupon the Guaican, like an arrow out of a bow, shoots the other fish, and then gathering the mouth of the bag on his head like a purse-net holds them so fast, that he lets not loose till hauled out of the water.

Here the Spaniards having dined on delicate fish, went on still Westward, and came to an uninhabited isle, but well stocked with geese, pelicans and ugly dogs that could not bark.

Giant Bones in Peru

Extract from Of the Original of the Americans, whence they came, when, how, and from what People Planted. Location: Peru

The Peruvians themselves give some small testimony (in their ancient records) of a few boats that landed of old upon their coasts, which where (as they say) mighty and cruel giants, committing much bloodshed, slaughtering the natives everywhere; and having subdued the whole country, built stately edifices, of which remain yet the ruins of some foundations, very artificial and costly. They also showed near Manta, and Puerto Viego, many huge bones they believe to be of giants, three times longer and thicker than an ordinary man's.

Winged Serpents Roasting near Mexico

Extract from The Expedition of Americas Vesputius (Amerigo Vespucci), circa 1497. Location: Gulf of Mexico

Having weighed anchor, and sailed eighty leagues along the coast, he ran into another convenient haven, whose shore swarmed with people, which on a sudden running away, hid themselves in a neighbouring wood.

Here the Spaniards landing were amazed, when in their huts they saw snakes and serpents roasting before a fire, whereof one had wings, and another whose mouth was tied together with a rope, stared with open eyes in a frightful manner.

AMERICUS VESPUTIUS

Sea-Spiders and Dragons in Sierra Leone

Extract from The Expedition of Americas Vesputius (1503). Location: Sierra Leone

His fourth expedition happened on May 10, 1503, at which time he steered directly with fix sail to Sierra Leone, and approaching the coast, could not come to an anchor, because of the strong eddying currents. Three degrees beyond the equinox appeared a rising island, two leagues long, and one broad, destitute of inhabitants, his best ship being six hundred tun, split here against a rock, and nothing of her was saved but the sea-men.

But Vesputius rowing ashore with a boat, found a convenient haven, with abundance of sweet water, high trees, sea-spiders, and horrible dragons. These dragons have a sharp head, round fiery eyes, and wide mouths, wings not unlike a bat's, a speckled breast, curled tail, blue back, and two bags like a drawn triangular satchel, were under their bellies.

No less strange are the sea-spiders, with their hard feet, long upper teeth, two long sheers or pinchers, and double belly. Between the head and the belly lies a black skin with which they darken the water; when anyone goes to take them in the night, they make a great shadow; they feed on fish, the female lays little white eggs, not unlike ordinary hail-stones.

Cabbages as Big as Trees near Panama

Extract from Peter Arias (Pedrarias Dávila) his Expedition, and Remarkable Passages of Vascus Nunnez (Vasco Núñez de Balboa). Location: in or near Panama

The Indian where the parrots are most frequent climbs into a tree, and chattering like them, with his voice imitating their notes, allures his fellow-prater to draw near, and be taken into his hands. But more belongs to the taking of wild fowl, as geese, ducks, swans, and the like: from the bottom of their standing pools and lakes in that country grow weeds, which spreading upon the water ripen, and rotting breed water-flies, spiders, and frogs, upon which the fowls feed.

Near these pools in the gardens grow cabbages as big as trees, which often dropping into the water serve the birds both for nests and food: but the skilful fowler finds it his best way to take one of these cabbages, and making it hollow in the middle, claps it on his head like a helmet, then going into the water up to his chin, and passing softly along in such manner, that nothing is seen but the floating cabbage, and coming near the birds, he takes them one after another by the legs, and puts them into a bag tied about his middle for that purpose.

But what is more worthy of observation is the American bird Toucan Xochitenachate, having a fleshy bill, like a mouth full of teeth, which continually opens and shuts to draw breath, having no nostrils; the back, neck, and wings, are black, the breast yellow like gold, the belly and end of the tail of a vermillion colour.

This bird Toucan feeds for the most part on pepper, which tarries not long with them, but muted almost as soon as swallowed: which pepper thus evacuated the natives value above their common, because the unpleasing sharp acidity, or biting quality is thereby much mitigated.

Bizarre Beast Sculptures and Idols in Yucutan, Mexico

Extract from The Expeditions of Francisco Fernandez, Lupus Caizedus, Christophero Morantes, Bernardo Igniguez, and Juan Grisalva. Location: Yucutan, Mexico

Six days the fleet had been at sea, when they discovered land, which by a mistake was called Jucatan (Yucatán), because the inhabitants being asked what was the name of the coast, answered "Jucatan"; which, as the Spaniards were afterwards informed, signified, "we understand you not".

In the city of Campechium, among other curious buildings, was a high, but square theatre of marble, on which stood the image of a man, on all corners assaulted by four wild beasts, which were of no less strange than horrible shape. Not far from this image they saw a serpent fashioned up of chalk and little stones, whose coiled up tail was forty seven foot long and of a proportionate thickness. This serpent, sprinkled with men's still warm blood, seemed to prey upon a marble lion: both these were enclosed with a stone rail, within which malefactors were daily executed. Bloody bows and arrows broken into small pieces lay between the bones and dead bodies.

Island of Sacrifice (near Tabasco, Mexico)

Extract from The Expeditions of Francisco Fernandez, Lupus Caizedus, Christophero Morantes, Bernardo Igniguez, and Juan Grisalva. Location: near Tabasco, Mexico

Soon after, they landed on the Island of Sacrifice, so called from the horrid sacrifices which the inhabitants made daily.

Amongst the other strange images, there stood a great lion of marble, seeming almost decollated with a great gash into which wound they poured human blood warm, which was received into a stone trough set for that purpose underneath; then the figure of a man carved in alabaster, bowing forward, as if looking into the trough upon the blood. Those which were sacrificed were prisoners taken on the neighbouring coasts, whom bringing before their idols, they ripping open make no farther inspection, but only to whip out the heart; with which having smeared the lips of their idols, they throw it into the fire: the heads and corps they let lie unburied; whose fleshy parts, especially their cheeks, they feast upon.

Ten-Foot Giant Ate My Biscuits

Extract from The Expedition of Ferdinand Magaglian, commonly called Magellane (1519) Location: Patagonia

Five months he plied up and down the coast inhabited by the Patagones, where he found none but a single person, or rather a monster, a giant ten foot high, who coming aboard his ship, devoured a great hamper of biskets, and at one draught drunk up nine pottels [*4.5 gallons*] of water.

FERDINAND MAGELLANUS.

Creeping Leaves in Borneo

Extract from The Expedition of Ferdinand Magaglian (1519) Location: Borneo

The chiefest island, called Borneo, hath two hundred fifty four leagues in circumference, whereon a tree grows, whose leaves when fallen off, seem to be alive and creep like worms.

Flesh Eating Unicorns near the US-Canada border

Extract from The Second Book, Containing a Description of Northern America, Sect. II New Netherland, now called New York (pub. 1671). Location: US-Canadian border

On the borders of Canada there is seen sometimes a kind of beast which hath some resemblance with a horse, having cloven feet, shaggy mane, one horn just on their forehead, a tail like that of a wild hog, black eyes, and a deer's neck: it feeds in the nearest wildernesses: the males never come amongst the females except at the time when they couple, after which they grow so ravenous, that they not only devour other beasts, but also one another.

Buffles Vomit Scalding Liquor when Hunted near New York

Extract from The Second Book, Chap. 1, Sect. II New Netherland, now called New York (pub. 1671). Location: south of New York

Towards the south of New York are many Buffles, beasts which (according to Erasmus Stella) are betwixt a horse and a stag: though they are of a strong constitution, yet they die of the smallest wound, and are subject to the falling sickness. They have broad branchy horns like a stag, short tail, rough neck, hair coloured according to the several seasons of the year, broad and long ears, hanging lips, little teeth, and skin so thick, as not easy to be pierced. The females differ from the males, for they have no horns. Both may easily be made tame. When hunted, they vomit out a sort of scalding liquor on the dogs; they have great force in their claws, for they can kill a wolf with the same at one blow. Their flesh, either fresh or salted, is a good diet. Their claws also cure the falling sickness.

[*Note: Falling sickness is an archaic term for epilepsy*]

Delicate Miniature Birds in New York

Extract from The Second Book, Chap. 1, Sect. II New Netherland, now called New York (pub. 1671).
Location: New York

Moreover, New York breeds a strange bird about a thumb long, full of glittering feathers; it lives by sucking of flowers like a bee, and is so tender, that it immediately dies if water being spirted upon it; the carcas being dried, is kept for a rarity.

Murderous Apes and Disappearing Plants in Guatemala

Extract from The Second Book. Chap IV Guatimala (published 1671).
Location: Chiapa, Guatemala

Guatemala stretches to the Isthmus, or Neck of Land, which joins the Northern and Southern parts of the New World together.

This country is bounded Northward with the Peninsula of Jucatt, and part of the Gulf or Bay of Honduras; on the South, with Mare del Zur; on the East and South-East, it has Castella Aurea and on the West, New Spain.

The length of it lies upon the Coast of Mare del Zur, and is said to be little less than three hundred Leagues; but the breadth not half so much, and in some places very narrow. It is generally a fertile and good country in all respects, but especially abounding in cattle and good pastures; it is subdivided into seven inferior provinces or countries, which are 1. Chiapa. 2. Verapaz. 3. Honduras. 4. Nicaragua. 5. Veragua. 6. Costa Rica; and 7. Guatemala, specially so called; all differing in language and customs one from another.

The Bishoprick (as it is now called) of Chiapa is bordered on the West with New Spain; on the East with Vera Paz; and on the South with Mare del Zur. It is country much shaded with woods, and those replenished with many fair and goodly trees, of diverse sorts, and of the largest size, as Oaks, Pines, Cedar, Myrtle and Cypress trees, besides others which yield them a good kind of Rozen, precious gums, etc. and also several sorts of Balsom, as white, red, green, and black, not only pleasant to the scent, but an excellent remedy for all manner of green wounds. The best of it drops out of the cut bodies of the trees; and the worst is pressed out of the wood and leaves.

There are also proper to this country several other kinds of trees and plant as that whose fruit tastes like pepper and cloves, being of a great height; a tree whose leaves cure all ulcerated sores, or the bitings of any poisonous beast.

There is a fort of cabbage called Ilantas, which grows to the height of a tree so that birds make their nests in them; they are eaten likewise like other common cabbages.

There is also an herb with narrow leaves, which is no sooner touched, but shrinks up to nothing; but at the going away of those which touch it, it obtains its former vigour.

Amongst the several forts of falcons which breed in this country, there is one sort which hath one foot proper to its kind, the other like that of a goose; it feeds on fish along the rivers.

The bird Toto-Queztall, which is somewhat smaller than a pigeon, with green feathers and a long tail, is taken only for its tail, which when the Indians have pulled out they let the bird fly again, there being a law amongst them, that whosoever kills one of them, is to suffer death.

The wild hogs which breed here have their navels on their backs, and have no tails, they smell exceeding strong, and feed together in great companies.

The Taquatrin, a certain beast proper to those pares, has a bag under its belly, in which it generally carries seven or more young ones, and has also a bald tail; it creeps into houses in the night to steal hens.

Here is also a certain beast (whose name we find not) about the size of a rabbit, and like a rat, and carries its young ones on its back whensoever it comes abroad.

The serpents, which are very numerous here, trouble the inhabitants exceedingly, especially near the village Ecatepeque, where there are such an abundance on two little hills, that none dares approach them; some of them are very poisonous, for if touched with a stick, the poison runs up the same: and whoever are anointed with the blood of a dead serpent, die a lingering death. John de Laet relates, that the Indians took one which carried thirty young ones, which being a finger long, crept up and down immediately; and the old one, being above twenty foot long, served the natives for venison.

Amongst other beasts is also the Teuthlacokauhqui, or fortress of the serpents; it has a head like an adder, thick belly, glittering scales, a black back, sprinkled with white crosses; at its tail there grows yearly a bone, with which it makes a noise when it stirs; its poisonous teeth destroy those which are bit therewith in twenty four hours, unless the part which is wounded be held in the earth so long till the pain be over. Notwithstanding the noise, terrible aspect, and gestures of this animal, the Indian hunters make nothing to take the fame by the tail, and wrap it up in linen, and carrying it home make it tame. It is able to live a whole year without either meat or drink; its head when cut off grows to the bigness of a man's thigh in ten days' time.

No less resolute are the Indians in taking the Ibitobaca, which is an ell long, of crimson colour, full of black and white specks, the bones whereof they wear about their necks instead of chains.

[*Note: An ell is a unit of measurement approximating the length of a man's arm from elbow to the tip of his middle finger. It is about 46cm*]

The Iquanna is a serpent which does no manner of hurt, though terrible to look upon to those which know it not, having a bag under its chin, a glittering comb on its head, and on its back sharp bones, which stand like a saw, and a long tail. It lays fifty eggs at a time as big as acorns, of a very good taste, and fit to eat when boiled. It also lives both in the water and on the land.

Here are also many baboons, which are big and heavy, with ugly heads, short legs like a man, and tails standing upwards; they eat all sorts of fruit, but chiefly covet after wine and bread; and are so lascivious, that they often set upon women. The females generally bring forth two, one male, and the other female. There is also another sort, whole skins, being red, are full of little spots.

...The chief place of the Quelenes is Copanavatzla, where there is good cheese, and store of brave cattle. The river Chiepa gliding through the midst thereof, loses itself in the Northern Ocean. In this part of the country are beasts not unlike apes, with long tails, which they wind about the legs of those whom they find swimming and so pull them under the water; wherefore they that go to swim take axes along with them, to cut off their tails.

Honey of Insanity and Bloot-Letting Danta in Vera Paz

Extract from The Second Book, Chap IV. Sect. II Vera Paz(published 1671).
Location: Vera Paz (now part of Guatemala)

Vera Paz, or The Country of True Peace, was so named by the Spaniards, as they say, because it was never conquered by the sword but reduced to obedience only by the preaching of the Dominican Friars. It is bounded on the West and South-West with Chiapa; on the East with some part of Guatemala and Honduras; and on the North with Yucatan. It contains about thirty Leagues in length, and almost as much in breadth, being a woody and mountainous country for the most part, yet well distinguished with valleys and lower ground.

It is much subject to rain, which it is said to have for nine months of the year almost continually; by reason whereof the country, being otherwise hot, is much annoyed with a kind of mosquito, or great fort of gnats, which spoil the fruit very much, and are otherwise not a little trouble to the people. Moreover, there happen oftentimes terrible earthquakes and storms, with thunder and lightning.

The chief commodities of this country, are a kind of amber, which some call Liquid Amber, which drops from diverse of their trees, and is said to be a commodity very precious, and of much use; Mastick, Sanguis Draconis, Gum Anime, Sarsaparilla, China-Wood, and diverse other medicinal drugs, which it has in great plenty. The woods afford a sweet smell, and the trees in the same grow a wonderful height.

The canes which grow here, being a hundred foot long, and proportionately thick, serve for timber.

There is also a hard wood called Iron Wood, either from its hardness or its colour, or both, which never rots.

The abundance of flowers which grow here afford nutriment to innumerable swarms of bees, which are about the size of small flies. Their honey, which is somewhat tart, they hide in the roots of trees, or in the earth. Another sort, which is made by the wasps, bereaves those that taste of their senses.

The noted beast in this country is the Danta, which resembles a mule, hath no horns, but ash coloured long hair, short neck, hanging ears, thin legs, with three claws before and two behind, long head, narrow forehead, little eyes, a nose hanging over its mouth, little tail, sharp teeth, and a skin which is six fingers thick, and scarce penetrable by any weapon. This beast is taken in traps, holes, or else with dogs, which he often kills when hunted towards the water. They say that this beast taught men first to let blood; for if it be too full of blood, it pricks itself against a sharp cane, and stops up the orifice again very carefully. The flesh thereof is good meat.

Giant Serpents and Bearded Fish in Mexico

Extract from The Second Book, Chap IV. Sect. V. Couliacan. (published 1671)
Location: Couliacan, Mexico

Next to Chiametla, Westward and Southward of Cinoloa, lies Couliacan, coasting all along the Bay of Califomia, which it has on the West ; on the East it has New Biscay; and on the South, Xalifco. The country is not defective in any kind of necessary provision, but more especially it abounds with fruits of all sorts. But the Spaniard look only at the mines, of which they have some few in this country. The people were generally clothed with cotton wool when the Spaniards came first among them.

This country was first discovered by Nunnez de Gusman (after he had built Guadalajara) after this manner: Marching from Chiametla to Piatzala, he ruined this province with fire and sword. He likewise conquered the countries of Zapuatun and Piaztla; the first being a plain, lay enclosed within high mountains, where the Spaniards met none but women, till they came to a great river called De La Sall, whose banks on each side were well inhabited the second juts against the ocean, and is watered by a river of the same denomination. Here, within the houses, (which are built after a strange manner) lay thousands of serpents mingled together, with their heads sticking out on the top and at the sides, and hissing with open mouth at those which approached them.

The inhabitants showed great reverence to these serpents, because (as they said) the devil often appeared to them in that form. And this seems to be a custom amongst them from the tradition of Eve being tempted by the devil in the shape of a serpent. Nor was this superstition peculiar only to these Indians, forasmuch as diverse nations of the ancient heathens of other parts of the world, worshipped the likeness of a serpent. And even amongst the Greeks, according to Plutarch, Hesychius, Clemens, Alexandrinus, and others, it was no unusual thing in their religious worship to call on Eve, and at the same time to show a serpent.

Plutarchus and Aetianus say, that the Egyptians honoured a serpent for their god. The same said Erasmus Stella of the old Prussions; Sigismund Baro, of the Lislanders; and Alexander Guaginus, of the Sarmatians and Samogethes. Moreover, some write, that in the province of Calecut are serpents with exceeding great heads, and weighing as much as a great hog, to which the king shows great reverence. So that it seems the Devil takes delight to be worshipped in that shape wherein he worked the fall of mankind.

Gusman leaving Piaztla marched to Bayla, where he found the great river De Mugeres, and the country full of woods and pastures. Thence travelling upwards along Mugueres, they ascended to the top of a mountain, where they were assaulted by the inhabitants of the village Quinola, whom nevertheless they soon put to flight; but not long after received a shrewd repulse at the entrance into a wood built full of houses; yet nevertheless being at length conquerors, though not without sufficient loss, they marched farther in amongst the mountains, till their provisions beginning to grow scarce, and they seeing no likelihood of getting to an end of this troublesome journey, at last their necessities forced them to retire.

The flood which comes out of the sea up to the city St. Michael, through the river Cignatlan, abounds with fish, and especially the Guarapucu, which is seven foot long when it comes to its full growth; it hath no scales, but a smooth skin of a silver colour mixed with green. From the head to the tail runs a crooked line of thin scales on each side; it swims exceeding swift, feeds on lesser fishes, and spawns in the sea. The flesh being wholesome and good to eat, is salted up against winter.

At the same place is also the Piracarba, which shines exceedingly, having silver-coloured scales, a broad slit tail, a long white beard, four great fins, and a little head. Farther into the sea are a sort of flying fish, called Pirabebes, which rise by thousands up out of the water, so escaping the dolphins and other fish which prey on them; yet sometimes they are snatched up by the birds, or else by the fishes, when they dive down into the water to wet their own wings, which consist of a thin skin, distinguished in length by tough fins. These flying fish also differ much one from another, for most of them are like herrings; others have a thick head, round before like the dolphins.

Reading by Fly-Light and Riding on Manatees in Hispaniola

Extract from The Second Book, Chapter XIII. Hispaniola. (pub. 1671)
Location: Hispaniola, Greater Antilles

The animals peculiar to this island are 1. A little beast called Hutias, not much unlike our Coneys. 2. Chemi, almost of the same form, but a little bigger. 3. Mohui, a beast somewhat less than the Hutias. 4. A beast called Coxi.

[Note: Coney is an old term for rabbit]

Likewise amongst other strange sorts of creatures here, the Cuyero is very observable, being about an inch big, and having four wings, of which two are larger than the other: when they fly they shine after such a manner, that in the night they make a room as light as day, insomuch that some have made use of them instead of candles to read by.

No less wonderful is the fish Manate. It breeds for the most part in the sea, yet sometimes swimming up the rivers, comes ashore and eats grass. The Casique Caramatexi kept one in the lake Guaynato which was so tame, that when called by the name Maton, it used to come out of the water, and go directly to the Casique's house, where being fed, it returned to the lake, accompanied with men and boys, who with their singing seemed to delight the fish, which sometimes carried ten children on its back over the water; but at last a Spaniard striking at it with a pike, it would never come forth again when it espied a clothed man. It lived twenty six years in the fore-mentioned lake, till by accident the river Hayboaic over-flowing into the said lake, the fish returned to the sea.

[Note: A Casique is a leader of an indigenous group or tribe]

Besides this great fish, here is also a sort of small fish, called Abacatuaia, with a little mouth, black eyes encompassed with silver-coloured circles, four black fins, two long ones under its belly, one on the back, and one on each side of the head, the tail slit and covered with a glittering skin. It is as big as a flounder, and not ill meat, but thick and round.

Numb Eels and Sleeping Apples in Guiana

Source P617. Extract from The Third Book, Containing a Description of Peruana or South America. Chap VIII. Guiana. Section II A Relation of the Journey of Francisco Orellana (pub. 1671)
Location: Guiana (a region that included Guyana, Suriname, French Guiana, and parts of Colombia, Venezuala and Brazil).

No plant is ever seen here without either leaf, blossom, or fruit, except the European apple tree , which never changes its nature, but blossoms and bears fruit at the same time of year as in Europe.

Some of the canoes made of the Trunks of Trees, will carry five or six tuns.

Each grain that is sown here produces in harvest above fifteen hundred.

The wild hogs Pokkiero, whose navels grow on their backs; and the Pangio, not unlike our swine, afford the inhabitants excellent food.

Here are also water-hogs of a very delicious taste; but because they are very apprehensive, and dive at the least noise, they are seldom taken.

The woods are full of Baboons and Apes, as also the slothful beast Ai.

The Hares here being of a brown colour, with white Specks, and the red rabbits, are accounted great delicacies.

There is no country in America, which breeds greater Armadillos, than Guiana, some of them weighing eighty pounds.

Here are also bears, which live on nothing but pismires; they have long hairy tails, with which they cover their bodies in rainy weather; they put their tongues a foot deep into the pismires nests, and so pulls them out.

[note: pismires is an archaic term for ants]

The Tygers here are either black, spotted, or red; but the black exceed the other in cruelty, yet are seldom seen near inhabited places; the spotted and red devour abundance of cattle but will seldom set upon a man, especially in the day-time.

The woods are also full of Land-Turtles, which the inhabitants take and keep till they have occasion to make use of their flesh.

The Eagles that are here with their claws, engage with those that go about to take them.

The Catamountains make such an exceeding noise at a certain hour, both in the night and in the day, that it is heard two Leagues off.

The Marmosets, a little beast, biting the Catamountains and Apes in the ears, forces them to leap from one tree to another.

The black beast Quotto has a face like an old Woman, and hanging by the tail, swings from one tree to another.

The Cuscary is a brown four-footed Creature, about the size of a little dog, but has the shape of a lyon.

Moreover, Guiana produces Teal, Geese, Cranes, Pheasants, Partridges, Pigeons, Marlins, Snipes, Falcons, Plovers, and Parrots of all sorts, besides many other strange fowls; amongst which the chiefest are a sort whose feathers glitter like scarlet, and walk along in rank and file like soldiers.

The Sea produces abundance of Turbots, Soles, Thornback, yellow Salmon, Sturgeon, Black-fish, Gurnets, Crabs, and Oysters. Amongst other fishes, the Caffoorwa, which is somewhat bigger than an eel, is very strange, having two sights in each eye, of which it always holds one above, and the other underneath the water when it swims.

Here are also the great fishes called Manati and Num-eel, by which if any part of a man be touched; it immediately becomes stiff.

There are likewise diverse vermine, which trouble the country Guiana, among which are serpents of thirty foot long, that come out of the water and feed on the land; they do little hurt, as not being poisonous: but there are many of a lesser size, whose biting is so venomous, that is causes the flesh of a man to rot in twenty four hours' time. Others there are which have forked tails, and tusks in the roof of their mouths.

The Crocodiles here also devour abundance of cattle.

The scorpions, which are black, and resemble a Lobster, breed under dry wood or corn; their stings are hid in their tails, with which if any one be touched, he is sure to endure an intolerable pain, but without danger of losing his life for the present, yet nothing can perfectly cure the same except the scorpion killed and laid on the wound.

The bats here are as big as pigeons, and they suck the blood of men and beasts so gently, that they seldom perceive the same.

Moreover, Guiana produces the gums Lemma, Barattu, and Carriman, which being black and prickly, smells very pleasantly, and cures the head-ache, bruises, pains in the limbs, gouts, and green wounds. The same operation has the gum Baratta.

Here are also good Sena, Bolus Armenius, Cassia-Fistula, Terra-Lemnia, the berry Kelette, very effectual against the bloody-flux, the juice of the leaf Upee, which cures the wounds of poisoned arrows, and a sort of somniferous apples, whereof the least bite occasions a deadly sleep.

There is also a tree, generally growing about the houses of the natives, the boughs whereof bruised between two stones, and thrown into the creeks of deep water full of fish, cause them to swim above water upon their backs.

Colour Changing Birds of St. Martin

Extract from The Second Book, Sect VII. St. Martin (pub. 1671)
Location: St. Martin

There are diverse pools of salt water in this island, which afford the inhabitants store of fish, and especially tortoises.

The woods produce Wild Hogs, Pigeons, Turtle-Doves, and Parraquito's resembling a parrot, and which though much smaller, are more apt to be taught.

Arber Papaya

Near the salt-pools also breed birds called Flammans, not unlike a Jack-daw, only differing in feathers, for they are first white, next ash-coloured, and at last turn red; they seldom fly or sit alone, but for the most part in great flocks in open places, and Moorish grounds; when some of them seek for their food under water, one of them stands sentinel, and on the least noise or appearance of a man, gives notice by chirping to the rest, who hereupon immediately flee away; those that shoot them lie commonly hid under an Ox hide.

About the same pools breed likewise the American Swallows, with crooked bills, feet like ducks, black bodies, white bellies, and long tails.

Soap Trees of St. Barts

Extract from The Second Book, Sect VIII. St. Bartholomew (pub. 1671)
Location: St. Barts

Near St Martin, at sixteen degrees, lies the island St. Bartholomew, which being about five leagues in circumference, is surrounded with rocks, and was first planted by De Poincy. It makes a delightful prospect, because of the many trees which grow on the same; amongst which the most noted are the soap-trees, whose wood makes the water lather, and washes as well as soap; but they are of two sorts, for in some this soapy quality is contained in a round yellow fruit, not unlike a plum; in others a white soft root supplies the office.

The little tree Canopia, out of whose bark drops a gum, grows also very pleasant, the body being divided into several branches; the leaves are discoloured, being underneath of a dark green, and of a brighter at the top; the flower consists of five leaves, and closes at last into a kind of cherry, full of yellow juice, and white pulp; it blossoms generally in October and December, and bears ripe berries the two following months. A fire being made about the tree causes the bark to crack, whereby it yields abundance of gum, chiefly used in medicine for its opening and loosening quality.

Likewise the Paretuve-Tree, which grows along by the sea-side and by pools, is sufficiently remarkable, for the boughs thereof grow downwards, twined and plaited together so thick, that in time of war they serve for bulwarks, and are the recesses of wild swine.

Moreover, on this island, as on all the other hereabouts, grow Calabash-Trees, which have thick boughs and oval leaves joined one to another, and bear every month fresh flowers and fruit, grey flowers, marked with green streaks and black spots, and fruit with hard shells, full of juicy meat and flat seeds, which being taken out serve for boxes, cups, or little dishes.

No less wonderful is the fish called the Sea Apple, whose brown skin is full of prickles, which when the fish dies fall off, nothing remaining but a white shell curiously embroidered with little holes.

On the banks, and near the rocks, grow also Sea-Trees, whose thickest bough putting forth still lesser and lesser branches, are plaited together very wonderfully and being all glazed as it were with salt-petre, seem greyish.

The Tool-Using Crabs of Tobago
Source Extract from The Second Book, Sect XXVII Tabago.
Location: Tobago

The next which comes in view is tabago, (so called, as some think, from the quantity of that drug there planted) eight leagues long and four broad, lying in the eleventh degree and fifteen minutes of Northern latitude, and hath many high Mountains full of Wood, out of which glide eighteen streams, which watering the plains fall into the Sea.

Captain Vitgeest coming to an anchor here, found a convenient Inlet on the East, and fresh water to fill his casks. Half a league from the shore rise five rocks, through which he sailed with his ships. Within the cliff opens a bay, into which runs a river well stored with fish. More Westerly lies a larger inlet, which receives two delightful streams. From the Western Promontory runs also a cliff Northward into the sea.

This island is easily known by high coasts which rise on the East side, and so grows lower by degrees. It is likewise made pleasant by many walks of trees.

The sea produces abundance of those sorts of fish which are common amongst us, besides tortoises, that lay their eggs in the sand.

The Cra-fish thereabouts are not much unlike Lobsters, have white and well tailed flesh, but hard to digest; they catch them in the night on sandy shelves with lighted torches.

The Crabs get their food very wonderfully here; for when they observe the Muscles or Oysters to gape for fresh air, they put stones between their shells so that the not being able to shut them, they pull out the fish with their claws.

The woods feed an innumerable company of beasts somewhat resembling hogs, (whose navels are on their backs), Oppusums, Javaris's, and Tatows, as also the Agouty's and Must-Rats.

The Agoutys's are of a dark brown colour, and have little tails, two teeth in their upper, and as many in their lower jaw - they make a noise as is they spoke crying *Couye*. If hunted by dogs, they run into hollow trees, out of which they are routed by smoke.

The great Musk-Rats are as big as a Rabbit, and like them live in holes made in the ground, but resemble an European Rat, only their skins are black, except one part of their bellies which are white. They smell so strong of musk, that it over-comes those that carry them.

Amongst the brambles breed also serpents of a green colour, two yards long and an inch thick, feeding on locusts and birds, which they take in their nests, but do no hurt to mankind.

But Tobago boasts chiefly of the Sassafras Tree, which resembles the Pine-Tree, has a firm and straight body, and on the top boughs spread like a crown, the bark of a dark colour and smooth, and smelling very sweet; the leaves thin, notched, and of a deep green, have also a delicate smell. The thinned roots appear above the ground, and are exceeding good to cure green wounds, stoppings and shortness of breath occasioned by colds.

The tobacco, by the Caribbeans call'd Y-ouli, planted among the fruit-trees, grows very plentifully here. It shoots up from a stringy root, bitter of taste, with a thick stalk, which shoots out boughs with great leaves, woolly underneath, and bears a kind of violet flower, which when dried, are succeeded by little cods full of black seed; and to prevent the over-growing of it, they cut off the top of the main stalk.

The bird Colibry, which is exceeding beautiful, makes his nest under the Tobacco-leaves.

The Sagovin of São Luís Island

Extract from The Third Book, Chap VII, Sect. X Maragnan (pub. 1671). Location: São Luís Island

Maragnan, forty five leagues in circumference, lies in two degrees of southern latitude.

...On the other side of the promontory Tapoytapere near Maragnan, towards the River of Amazones, lie so many isles along the sea-shore, that no ship is able to approach the same, because the spaces between the isles are overgrown with trees called Apparituriers, whose boughs shooting down and rooting in the sea, produce other trees, which grow so close together, that they seem one entire tree with many branches. Besides this inconvenience there is abundance of drift sand when the wind sits from the shore, which oftentimes swallows the ships which lie upon the same.

The ocean about Maragnan produces abundance of all sorts of fish, and amongst others the Pyraon, six foot long, thicker than a barrel, and covered with black scales of a hand-breadth.

The fish Camouroupouy differs not much from the Pyraon, only in having fewer scales.

The Ougry, four foot long, has a broad head, and two sharp fins on the back, which wound terribly. This fish also swimming in the river, smells of musk whilest it stays therein.

The like length has also the Camboury Ouassou, whose hog-like head, and yellow scaled tail, makes it seem like a monster.

The Lauebouyre is a foot in thickness, in length two fathom, and a fathom in breadth, and hath a tail of half a fathom long, out of the middle of which flicks a sharp and great bone, which makes such dangerous wounds, that if any part of a man's body be touched therewith, it must be cut off.

The Narinnary, which is much lesser, wounds with its sting very dangerously.

The flat fish Acaraiou has the length of a foot, a green head, thick scales, a yellow back, and white belly. The Araououa has a hard skin, is eight times bigger than the Acaraiou, and has a three-pointed sword, with which it kills other fish. Another sort of sword-fish is the Panapans, whose sword is a foot less than that of the Araououa.

The rivers and brooks on Maragnan are also very full of fish, amongst which the Pourake, four foot long, full of green, blue, red and white specks and streaks; the skin so hard that no sword can penetrate it; wherefore it regards not a blow, but if it moves, it causes such a pain on the arm of him that strikes, that he falls down on the ground.

The Caurimata, which is very like a Carp, is the most delicious fish that ever was tasted.

The Pyrain, without Scales, coloured red and yellow, has sharp teeth, which cut slopingly, as also the Opean, Tarehure, Paraty, and Jerou.

The red crabs Ouffa, with hairy legs, breed about the roots of the forementioned trees that grow in the eater.

The white crabs Aouara-ouffa carry the Ambergris, cast on the shores to their holes.

Moreover, this island feeds abundance of four-footed beasts, amongst which their wild deer, rabbits and hares, differ little from the European. They have also wild swine called Taiassou, who seem to have navels on their backs, which cast a sweet musky smell; besides another sort of swine, not inferior to the former, but of a stranger shape, being mouthed like a hare, with two long tusks in their upper jaws, and two beneath; their ears like a man's; the foremost feet white, and hooved like an ass; the hindermost part of their body like a bear, and full of bristles, half white and half black, three handfuls long. When they creep in their holes their staring bristles fall; they keep much amongst brambles, feed on apple; and roots; in the winter season they stye themselves up in their holes.

Here are also pismire [ant] eaters, called Tamandua, with a boars head, dogs ears, sharp snout, horses hair, and ox feet.

The Tapiyre-ete differ little from wild cows, only they have shorter legs and tails, and wanting horns, are armed instead thereof with teeth; in their head are often found a stone like the Bezoar stone.

[Note: Bezoars are hard, stone-like masses of indigestible material formed in the stomach of some animals. They were historically valuable objects as they were believed to have the power of a universal antidote against any poison.]

Here is also a deformed slow creeping beast called Ai, whose head is like a man's and covered with rough and grey hair, on each foot three claws close together and at least a finger long, sharp teeth, a smooth high black nose, little drowsing eyes, no ears, a tail small above and broad at the bottom, long ash-coloured hair over all the body; and being about the bigness of a fox, it climbs slowly up the trees, and comes not down before it hath eaten off all the leaves; it feeds also on earth, and sometimes sits on a high bough without meat twenty days together - it goes so softly, that it will hardly clear fifty paces in twenty four hours.

On this island are likewise all sorts of apes and monkeys, amongst which is one most remarkable, called the Zimme Cayon, hairy all over, with a long white beard, an old man's face, bald ears, black eyes and long tail, which they wind about a bough, and so hanging, swing themselves from one tree to another. They are very fierce as well as subtle, for being wounded with an arrow, they set upon the enemy without the least fear. When they climb up the trees, they carry their mouths and hands full of stones to throw at travellers; and if any one of them chance to be wounded, all the rest that are near come to help him, and stop the wound with leaves, and the like. The young ones hang upon the backs of the dams, who run very swift with them, and leap from one tree to another.

Juan Ardenois relates, that the coyons play at certain games with the natives for money, and spend what they win in public houses.

Joseph de Acofta tells us, that one of these kind of creatures being sent to a tavern for wine, would not part with his money before his pot was filled, which he defended from the boys that offered to take it from him, by throwing stones at them; and though it loved wine very well, yet brought it always home without tasting.

It is no less wonderful what Peter Martyr relates of one of these creatures, viz. that observing one ready to fire a gun at him, before he could discharge, it leaped from the tree and snatched up a child, which he held as a buckler [*shield*] before him.

The Sagovin resembles a lion in the fore-part of the body, with shaggy hair. They are exceeding dainty and tender, yet so stubborn and sullen, that they take pet at the least affront, and often pine themselves away and die with hunger.

Sources

All extracts are from the three books contained in the below publication.

AMERICA:

Being the Latest and Most Accurate Description of the New World; containing

The Original of the Inhabitants, and the Remarkable Voyages thither.

The Conquest of the Vast Empires of Mexico and Peru, and Other Large Provinces and Territories with the Several European Plantations in those Parts.

Also Their Cities, Fortresses, Towns, Temples, Mountains, and Rivers.

Their Habits, Customs, Manners, and Religions.

Their Plants, Beasts, Birds, and Serpents.

with An Appendix, containing, besides several other considerable Additions, a brief Survey of what has been discovered of the Unknown South-Land and the Arctic Region.

Collected from most Authentic Authors, Augmented with later Observations, and Adorned with Maps and Sculptures, by John Ogilby.

1671

AMERICA:

BEING THE LATEST, AND MOST

ACCURATE DESCRIPTION

OF THE

NEVV VVORLD;

CONTAINING

The Original of the Inhabitants, and the Remarkable Voyages thither.

THE CONQUEST OF THE VAST

EMPIRES

OF

Mexico and Peru,

AND OTHER LARGE

PROVINCES and TERRITORIES,

WITH THE SEVERAL *EUROPEAN*

PLANTATIONS

IN THOSE PARTS.

ALSO

Their Cities, Fortreſſes, Towns, Temples,
Mountains, and Rivers.

Their Habits, Cuſtoms, Manners, and Religions.

Their Plants, Beaſts, Birds, and Serpents.

WITH

An *APPENDIX*, containing, beſides ſeveral other conſiderable
Additions, a brief Survey of what hath been diſcover'd of the
Unknown South-Land and the *Arctick Region.*

49 Pls.

Collected from moſt Authentick Authors, Augmented with later Obſervations, and
Adorn'd with Maps and Sculptures, by *JOHN OGILBY* Eſq; His
Majeſty's *Coſmographer, Geographick Printer,* and Maſter of the *Revels*
in the Kingdom of *IRELAND.*

LONDON,
Printed by the Author, and are to be had at his Houſe in
White Fryers, M. DC. LXXI.

www.ingramcontent.com/pod-product-compliance
Lightning Source LLC
Chambersburg PA
CBHW050841290526
45792CB00001B/489